Meow Te Ching

Meow Te Ching

by Meow Tzu

The Way to Contentment, Serenity, and Getting What You Want

As Told to Michael Kent

Gramercy Books

New York

This 2001 edition is published by Gramercy Books™,
an imprint of Random House Value Publishing, Inc.,
280 Park Avenue, New York, New York 10017,
by arrangement with Andrews McMeel Publishing.

Gramercy Books™ and design are trademarks of
Random House Value Publishing, Inc.

Random House
New York • Toronto • London • Sydney • Auckland
http://www.randomhouse.com/

Printed and bound in the United States of America

A CIP catalog record for this book is available from the Library of Congress.

ISBN 0-517-16344-6

8 7 6 5 4 3 2 1

Contents

Loved by his followers, respected by his ene-mies, and adored by the opposite sex, Meow Tzu is probably the most famous cat to have ever lived. Yet most humans know little about him. Cats have kept his name a secret, waiting for the darkest hour, when people are asleep, to pass on his wisdom from generation to generation.

Recently, however, a small group of intellectuals at some of the world's greatest universities— Harvard, Stanford, Beijing, the Sorbonne—have become aware of this remarkable cat. Archaeological digs near the Dead Sea, Machu Picchu, and Tibet have unearthed a number of manuscripts, notes taken by disciples of the venerable Meow.

These ancient manuscripts, with their beautiful paw prints and scrawls, reveal a cat that was at once a leader with keen insight into feline nature, a philosopher profoundly aware of the tragedy of existence, and a revolutionary with a vision of equality in which no cat would be a stray. In addition, Meow Tzu was a mystic, communicating the way to a peaceful—even blissful—existence.

People have long recognized the spiritual nature of cats. Serene and self-reliant, they have a way of living in the moment, of remaining detached from transient events, of being centered and at peace. Perhaps, with the discovery of *Meow Te Ching*, we will understand more about the secrets of feline enlightenment.

Many of Meow's sayings seem oddly familiar to the human reader. For example, "The journey of a thousand miles begins with a single stretch," and "You can't have your mouse and eat it too." This is the subject of much debate. Is it because there is an invisible world of ideas, accessible to both people and cats? Or is it because cats have had a far greater effect on human history than we ever imagined, somehow transmitting important ideas to the people they love?

We may never have definitive answers to these questions, but the proverbs in this brief collection are certain to help humans learn more about their feline friends. Moreover, Meow's gentle wisdom and piercing wit transcend barriers of species and time, giving people the opportunity to learn a thing or two about themselves.

Although his wisdom surpasses nine lives— "Yea, ninety lives," say his followers—some believe that the "Great Cat" is alive again today. Meow sightings have been reported from the jungles of Peru to the windswept plains of Africa, from the foothills of

Nepal to backyards in Boston. None of these have been authenticated, but they present the exciting possibility that we could learn even more about this legendary figure.

Presently, however, let us make the most of the remarkable discoveries that scholars have pieced together so far. In Meow's words, "When fortune reaches out her paw, seize it."

Michael Kent
Pacific Grove, California

MEOW

THE

LEADER

虎

What makes a cat a great leader? Is he born with this gift, or can the skills of leadership be learned?

While Meowists and other scholars will probably debate these questions for many years, they all agree that Meow Tzu was one of the most extraordinary leaders of his time. He had a way of bringing out the best in others, even without saying a word. His very presence commanded excellence.

Perhaps this is because Meow practiced what he preached. Well-groomed, in perfect condition, he never called on his followers to do anything that he was not willing to do himself. Whether charging into battle, defending the truth, or going the extra mile for a stray, he always set a motivating example. "One brave deed is worth a thousand meows," he often said.

His followers remember many pleasant evenings when, after savoring a meal of field mice or fish, Meow would talk to them about wisdom and virtue. "Felines," he would say, "I know you can't be perfect, but acting with courage is what life is all about. I promise, if you make every effort to be true to your heritage, to awaken the lion within, your lives will be more prosperous than you ever imagined."

Meow loved his fellow cats, and they could feel his love. Because of this, they wanted to live up to his expectations, they wanted to prove themselves worthy of his affection and confidence. He believed in them, and this helped them to believe in themselves.

Here, then, are some of Meow's most cherished and inspirational sayings that reveal his secrets of leadership.

虎

The journey of a
thousand miles
begins with a
single stretch.

虎

If you itch for
something,
go scratch for it.

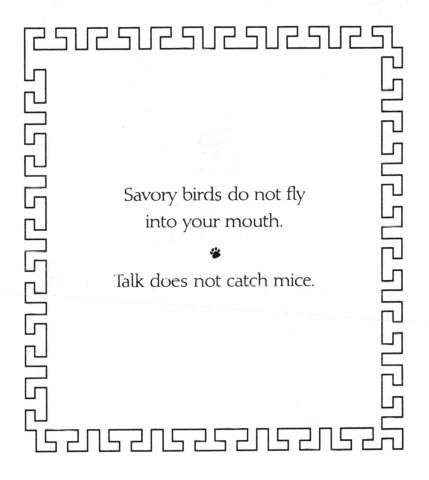

Savory birds do not fly
into your mouth.

🐾

Talk does not catch mice.

虎

When fortune reaches out her paw, seize it.

You'll never catch a mouse
by chasing it in your mind.

If you are afraid of getting wet,
you will never be good
at catching fish.

Whatsoever thy paw findeth to do,
do it with all thy might.

The early cat
catches
the early bird.

One brave deed is worth
a thousand meows.

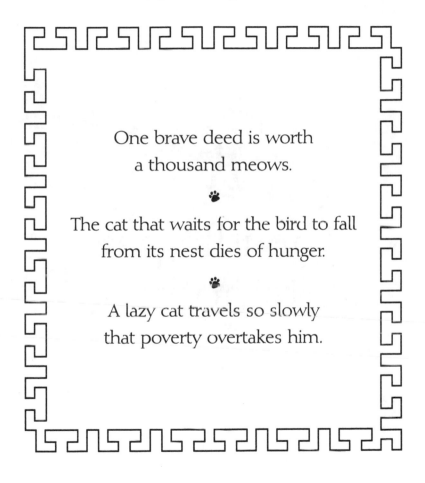

The cat that waits for the bird to fall
from its nest dies of hunger.

A lazy cat travels so slowly
that poverty overtakes him.

虎

The idle paw gets nothing.

貓

Hesitate too long
and, behold,
another cat
will take away
your supper.

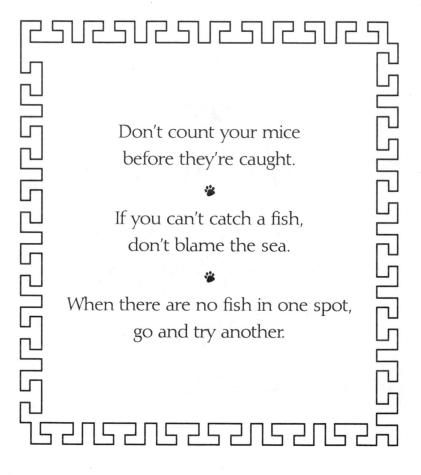

Don't count your mice
before they're caught.

If you can't catch a fish,
don't blame the sea.

When there are no fish in one spot,
go and try another.

虎

Sometimes you
must step back
in order to make
a better leap.

虎

It is not enough
for a cat to know
how to climb;
he must also
know how to fall.

No matter
how far you have
traveled down
the wrong road,
turn back.

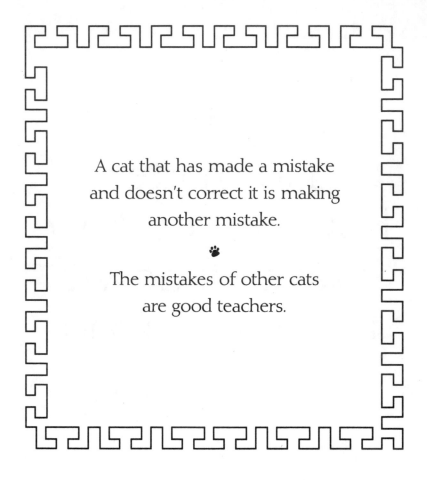

A cat that has made a mistake
and doesn't correct it is making
another mistake.

The mistakes of other cats
are good teachers.

虎

I don't think much of the cat that is not wiser today than he was yesterday.

虎

Give a cat a fish
and you feed him
for a day;
teach a cat to fish
and you feed him
for a lifetime.

See that you are wise, but also
learn how to appear ignorant.

If you want to fool,
pretend to be a fool.

Nothing is so full of victory
as patience.

When a cat is a great leader, his
followers say, "We did it ourselves."

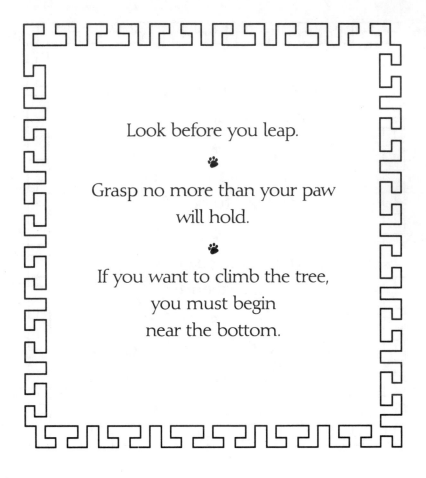

Look before you leap.

❖

Grasp no more than your paw
will hold.

❖

If you want to climb the tree,
you must begin
near the bottom.

Consider your
opponent a wolf,
not a mouse.

The cat that goes softly
goes safely.

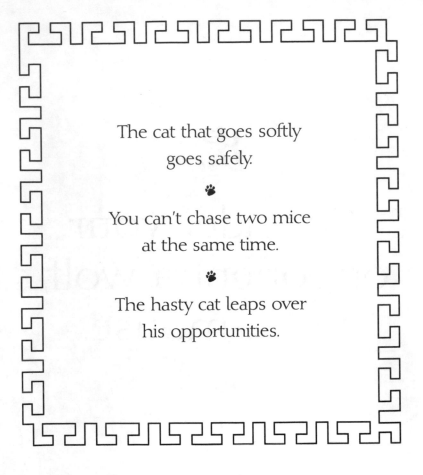

You can't chase two mice
at the same time.

The hasty cat leaps over
his opportunities.

虎

Hasty climbers have sudden falls.

虎

Walk fast and you catch misfortune; walk slowly and it catches you.

Silence catches
the mouse.

🐾

The foolish cat sees the gain,
not the danger.

🐾

The cat that loves danger
shall perish in it.

虎

The cat that
seeks trouble
always finds it.

If you can't bite,
don't show your teeth.

❧

Beware of the cat
with nothing to lose.

❧

Don't put your affairs
in the paws of a cat
that has failed to manage his own.

Cats who are once found to be bad are presumed to be so forever.

🐾

Keep bad cats' company and you'll soon be of their number.

🐾

A cat is known by the company he keeps.

虎

The cat that fights
and runs away
will live to fight
another day.

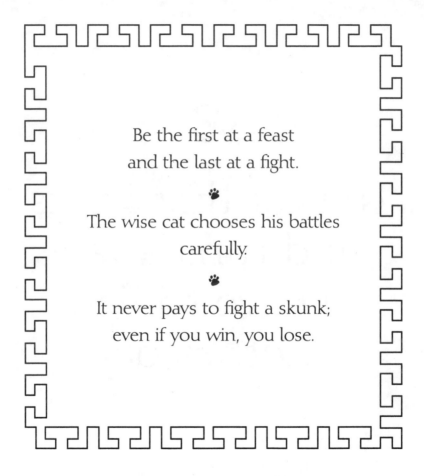

Be the first at a feast
and the last at a fight.

The wise cat chooses his battles
carefully.

It never pays to fight a skunk;
even if you win, you lose.

MEOW

THE

PHILOSOPHER

While Meow Tzu was a cat of action, he was also a profound thinker, endlessly seeking answers to life's most important questions. What is the meaning of a cat's life? How can she best live? Why should he be good?

Although Meow had a joyous heart, full of compassion ("No cat is poor that can purr," he said), he was acutely aware of the tragedy of feline existence: "A kitten cries when it is born, and every day explains why."

Like Confucius and Aristotle, the "Sage of Siam"—as his disciples sometimes called him— apparently never wrote down his own thoughts. Rather, we know him through the copious notes taken by his eager students. We are fortunate, indeed, to have this record, which reveals a great deal.

Because he was interested in a broad range of subjects—from logic and epistemology to metaphysics and ethics—Meow's philosophy is endlessly interesting, but it is also difficult to classify. Like other great thinkers, he sometimes contradicted himself, which is likely to have academics splitting whiskers for many years to come.

Here, then, are some of Meow Tzu's most provocative thoughts on the meaning of feline existence.

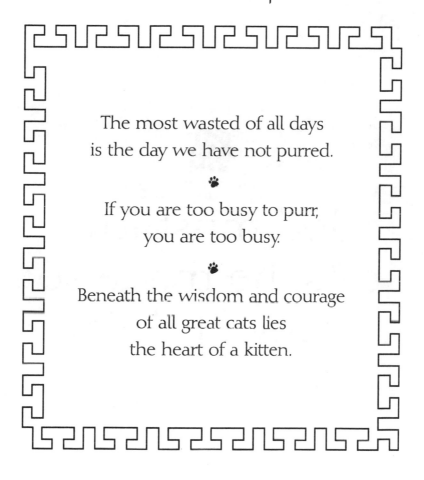

The most wasted of all days
is the day we have not purred.

If you are too busy to purr,
you are too busy.

Beneath the wisdom and courage
of all great cats lies
the heart of a kitten.

God must love cats; he made so many of them.

You can't have your mouse and eat it too.

A kitten cries
when it is born,
and every day
explains why.

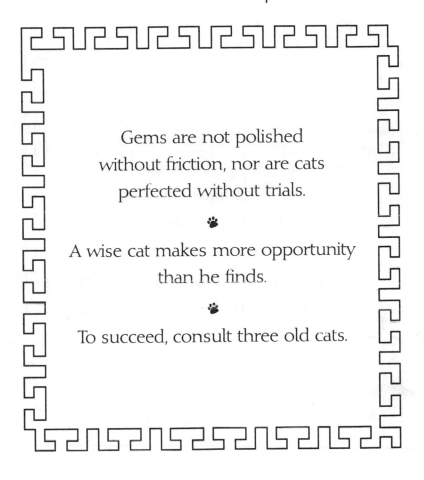

Gems are not polished
without friction, nor are cats
perfected without trials.

A wise cat makes more opportunity
than he finds.

To succeed, consult three old cats.

Some cats are born great,
some achieve greatness,
and some have greatness
thrust upon them.

❧

The wise cat, even when he is silent,
says more than the fool
when he speaks.

The silent cat
is often worth
listening to.

Learning is a treasure that follows
a cat everywhere.

Who is wise? He who learns
from all cats.

Anger is a thorn
in one's paw.

貓

When two cats
fight for a mouse,
a third runs away
with it.

It is usually the
reply that causes
the fight.

Quarrelsome cats get dirty coats.

❧

A cat should rule his passions,
or his passions will rule him.

❧

If heaven drops a bird from its nest,
open your mouth.

Pray to God for
a scrumptious
mouse, but
continue to hunt.

Pray to God for safety, but stay away
from the wolf.

Birds are given, but they are not
plucked for us.

When the fox makes
a speech, ponder
carefully what he says.

A ragged coat may cover a noble cat.

Beauty is fur deep.

Let every cat attend
to his own cleaning and
not worry about the dirt
on his neighbor's coat.

❧

Making a show of oneself is a
necessary art of living.

❧

An uneasy conscience
is like a hair ball in your throat.

貓

Purr and the
world purrs
with you;
weep and you
weep alone.

虎

Cats grow old,
pearls grow yellow—
there's no cure
for it.

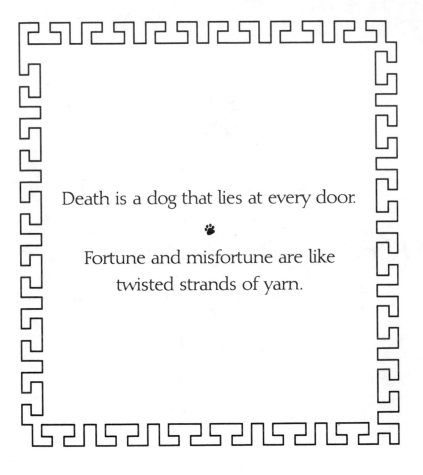

Death is a dog that lies at every door.

Fortune and misfortune are like
twisted strands of yarn.

貓

Time is a whisker on the face of eternity.

Do not blame
God for creating
dogs, but thank
him for not giving
them wings.

MEOW

THE

ROMANTIC

虎

Also known as *El Amoroso*, Meow Tzu had a way with the fairer of the species. Female cats adored him, and he returned their adoration. Stories of his affairs are many, and he seems to have had lovers on every continent.

Although he was not particularly handsome, Meow had a certain charisma, an underlying courage and strength, that females found irresistible. He was also sensitive to their feelings, and he had a way of making them feel special and alive. "All female cats are beautiful," he told one of his followers; "it is up to you to make them feel that way."

Meow's most dramatic affair was with a Himalayan that helped him recover after he was injured in a battle for feline freedom. Meow told his followers that this beautiful cat was "the love of his lives." She helped him regain his strength and, in his darkest hour, she probably saved him. Like the nurse who stole Hemingway's heart in an Italian hospital during World War I, this Himalayan inspired some of Meow's most poetic work.

At the touch of love,
every cat is a poet.

❧

No road seems long
when a cat goes
to meet his lover.

❧

When a cat is in love, the smallest
distance is too great, and the greatest
distance not too far.

虎

Love and health
are a cat's best
wealth.

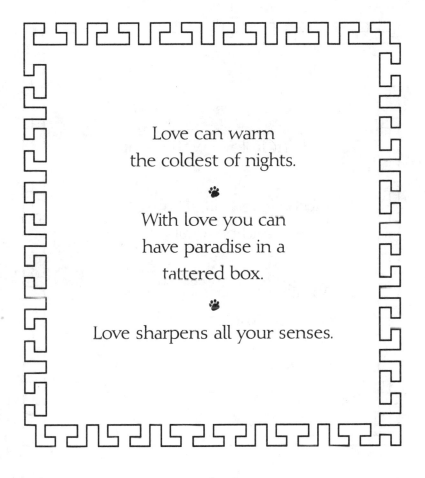

Love can warm
the coldest of nights.

With love you can
have paradise in a
tattered box.

Love sharpens all your senses.

I am in love with loving.

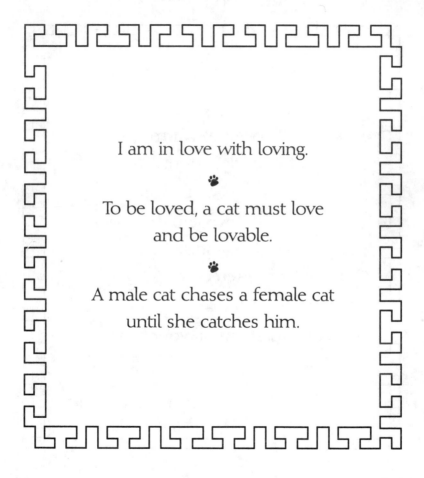

To be loved, a cat must love
and be lovable.

A male cat chases a female cat
until she catches him.

虎

A faint heart
never won
a fair feline.

No one acts more foolishly than
a wise cat in love.

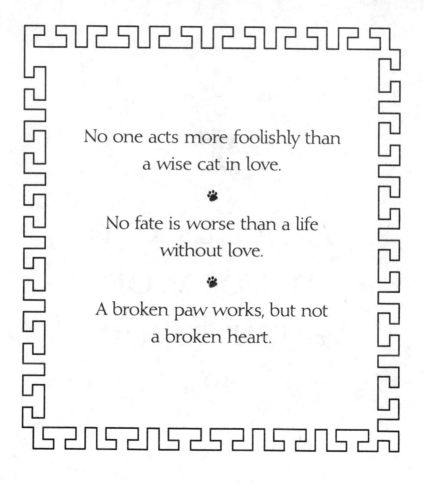

No fate is worse than a life
without love.

A broken paw works, but not
a broken heart.

虎

It is easy to
halve the fish
where there
is love.

Fear less, hope more;
eat less, chew more;
sigh less, purr more;
hate less, love more;
and all good things are yours.

🐾

All female cats are beautiful;
it is up to you
to make them feel that way.

MEOW

THE

MYSTIC

Many readers find Meow Tzu's mystical sayings to be his most inspiring and insightful. While he was often a pragmatist, Meow was able to go beyond the rational to embrace a world beyond this world, a reality beyond this reality, and he invites us to join him.

Shakespeare once observed, "There are more things in heaven and earth . . . than are dreamt of in your philosophy." Meow would concur. There are many things that we cannot understand by reason alone; we must trust our hearts, our intuition, if we are to begin to know what life is about.

Meow offers a way to a serenity and happiness. His students called this way "the eternal Meow."

The key, it seems, is to take time each day to be quiet and at peace—something that cats have learned well. Also, it is important to be detached from the things of this world and to be centered from within—another lesson that cats, through the ages, have clearly mastered.

貓

The things of this
world are passing;
if a cat clings to
them, it will be
a source of pain.

A cat must take time every day
to sit quietly and listen.

❧

The only way to bring
peace to earth is to learn
how to make your own life
peaceful.

No one
outside yourself
can rule you
inwardly.
When you know
this, felines,
you become free.

The cat that knows others
is clever, but the cat that
knows himself is enlightened.

❧

The wise cat travels all day
without leaving home.
How splendid are the views,
for she stays serenely in herself.

It is not a
cat's position,
but her disposition,
that gives peace.

Felines, if you cannot find the truth where you are right now, where must you go to find it?

The highest purpose is to have
no purpose.

❧

The wise cat realizes
that whatever he
possesses he will lose.

❧

Fortune takes from a cat only what
she has given to him.

The wise cat,
like the clouds,
receives only
to give away.

Always put a certain amount of play
into your work, and work
into your play.

When you play, just play;
when you eat, just eat;
when you rest, just rest.
Be present in the moment.

A cat that is not at peace
with the Creator cannot be at peace
with himself. He that is not at peace
with himself—how can he be
at peace with his neighbor?

❧

When you see a good cat,
think of emulating him;
when you see a bad cat,
examine your own heart.

The first part of the night,
felines, think of your own faults;
the latter part, think of
the faults of others.

❀

Beware of no cat more than thyself.

❀

If you kick dirt on another cat,
you will get dirty too.

貓

The cat that
loses himself in
love finds
himself at one
with the Creator.

MEOW

THE
REVOLUTIONARY

虎

Some of the manuscripts unearthed by archaeologists refer to Meow Tzu as "Chairman Meow." In one or more of his lives, it appears that he was a great revolutionary, a champion of feline rights and a defender of feline freedom.

While Meow loved many people and considered them to be his friends, he had little tolerance for any kind of chauvinism or tyrannical behavior. He taught his followers a method of civil disobedience, wherein they would not cooperate with anyone who treated them unfairly and without dignity. They were taught to resist such oppression, if possible, with courage and nonviolence.

In addition, Meow warned his fellow cats of

the dangers of a "soft life." He seemed to fear that they would lose touch with their proud heritage as hunters and survivors, choosing a life of comfort and security wherein all their needs were provided for by humans. Meow saw this as a fate worse than death, and he called on his brothers and sisters to "awaken the tiger within."

Give me liberty, or give me
my next life!

❀

It is better for a cat to die with honor
than to live in disgrace.

❀

Lean liberty is better than fat slavery.

A prison made of
pillows and lace
is still a prison.

It is not the
size of the cat
in the fight, but
the size of the
fight in the cat,
that makes
a difference.

Speak softly and carry sharp claws.

❖

A bold heart is half the battle.

❖

The coward dies a thousand deaths,
the brave just nine.

虎

Ask not what
your cat can do
for you, ask what
you can do for
your cat.

To err is human.

❖

It is human nature to think wisely
and act foolishly.

❖

It is harder to change human nature
than to move rivers or mountains.

❖

Human, train thyself!

虎

People are all
alike; they just
have different
faces so you can
tell them apart.

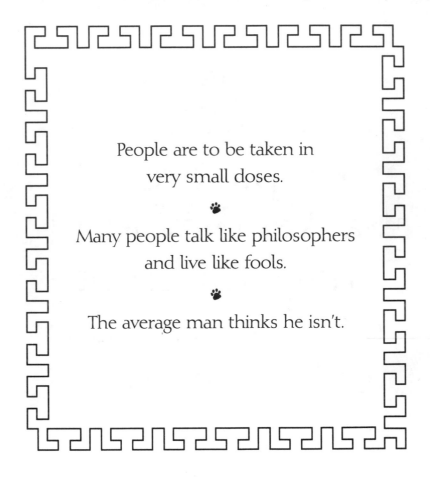

People are to be taken in
very small doses.

❧

Many people talk like philosophers
and live like fools.

❧

The average man thinks he isn't.

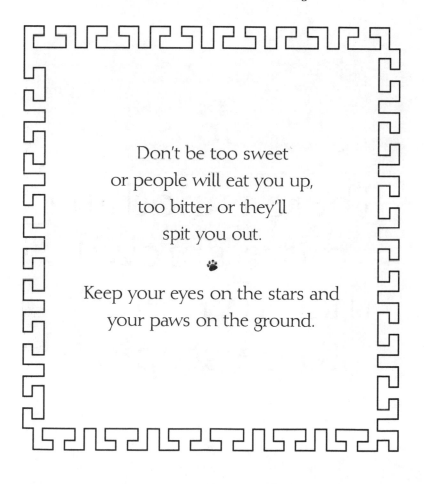

Don't be too sweet
or people will eat you up,
too bitter or they'll
spit you out.

Keep your eyes on the stars and
your paws on the ground.

There is nothing more shrewd than to pretend to be stupid.

Cunning surpasses strength.

A little cleverness counts for more
than great scholarship.

❧

Three things are best to avoid:
a strange dog, a flood,
and a person who thinks
he is wise.

❧

You can lead a person to reason, but
you can't make him think.

虎

Don't rejoice
over the
person who goes
before you see
he who comes.

A change of rulers is the joy of fools.

❧

Care about people's approval and
you will be their prisoner.

❧

The reputation of nine lives
may be determined by the conduct
of a single hour.

虎

No one can
walk over me
unless I
lie down first.

The way to be safe is to never
feel secure.

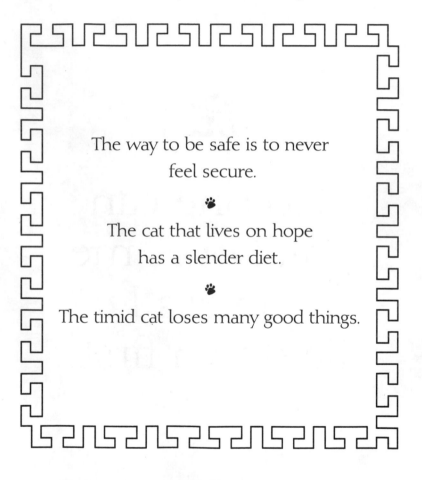

The cat that lives on hope
has a slender diet.

The timid cat loses many good things.

虎

Nine lives cannot
repair a moment's
loss of honor.

虎

Dogs that bark at a distance never bite.

It is enough to hiss
at a beaten dog.

You can't keep a good cat down.

Those cats can
that think they can.

虎

Sneak and ye shall find.

The sleeping cat will not catch a rat.

The mouse that knows but one hole
will soon be caught.

虎

Curiosity has killed more mice than cats.

RANDOM MEOWISMS

Some of Meow Tzu's thoughts are difficult to classify, yet they are favorites with cats on every continent, memorized by kittens worldwide. More than a revolutionary, he was the complete cat, and he had something profound to say on almost every conceivable subject.

Central to all of Meow's sayings, however, is the idea of being good to one another. He envisioned a circle of kindness, wherein all of our thoughts and actions have an effect on the world and ultimately on our own lives. "Your kindness to cats returns to you in the end," he said.

Meow envisioned a world in which cats and humans alike strive to be their best and to live good lives. To this end, he encourages his followers to seek wisdom and self-knowledge. He also reminds them to be practical, with their paws firmly planted on the ground, and to make the most of each and every day.

Better a
small fish
than an
empty dish.

A minnow in the paw is better than
a salmon in the sea.

❧

A bird in the paw is worth two
in the bush.

❧

Every fish that gets away
appears to be great.

Cleanliness is next to godliness.

A bashful beggar
has an empty dish.

'Tis better than riches
to scratch where it itches.

Once bitten, twice shy.

貓

Throw a lucky cat
into the river
and he will rise
with a fish
in his mouth.

貓

To bring up
kittens in the way
they should go,
travel that way
yourself.

You can never appreciate
your parents' love until you have
kittens of your own.

Good things come in
small packages.

The kitten that cries gets the milk.

虎

Learning is like climbing a tree: If you do not advance, you drop back.

貓

It is always
the ones that
meow the loudest
who do the least.

Even rest makes a lazy cat tired.

🐾

The cat that has the right to boast
doesn't have to.

🐾

Mingle a little folly
with your wisdom.

No cat is poor that can purr.

The mouse in its hole is a king.

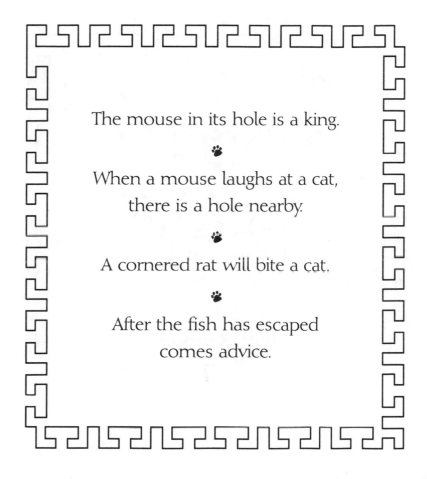

When a mouse laughs at a cat,
there is a hole nearby.

A cornered rat will bite a cat.

After the fish has escaped
comes advice.

I never met a cat I didn't like.

❦

Many paws make light work.

❦

One must scratch cats
where they itch.

❦

Put your best paw forward.

The cat that begins with patience ends with pleasure.

How beautiful it is to do nothing,
and then to rest afterward.

❖

Don't put off till tomorrow
what can be put off
till the day after tomorrow.

❖

Early to bed, early to rise, makes a cat
mighty tired by afternoon.

Cheerful company shortens the miles.

To those cats that are
good to me, let me be good;
to those that are not good to me,
let me also be good; thus shall
goodness increase.

🐾

You do not know who your friend is
until you fall into the stream.

One enemy is too many,
and a hundred friends
too few.

Your friend is the cat
who knows all about you,
and still likes you.

Your kindness
to cats
returns to you
in the end.